DATE DUE

MAY 18			

HIGHSMITH 45-112

Grant:

Jim Bridger,the
Mountain Man

★★★★★★★★★★★★★★★★★★★★★★★★★★★★★★★★

FRONTIERSMEN OF AMERICA

Jim Bridger

THE MOUNTAIN MAN

MATTHEW G. GRANT
Illustrated by Nancy Inderieden

GALLERY OF GREAT AMERICANS SERIES

★★★★★★★★★★★★★★★★★★★★★★★★★★★★★★★★

Jim Bridger

THE MOUNTAIN MAN

Library of Congress Number: 73-10071   ISBN: 0-87191-254-6

Published by Creative Education, Mankato, Minnesota 56001

Library of Congress Cataloging in Publication Data
Grant, Matthew G.
  Jim Bridger the mountain man.
                        (Gallery of great Americans)
  SUMMARY: A brief biography of the nineteenth-century trapper, scout, and explorer who helped open the west to settlers.
  1. Bridger, James 1804-1881—Juvenile literature. [1. Bridger, James, 1804-1881. 2. The West—Biography] I. Title. F592.B8544 978'.02'0924 [B] [92] 73-10071 ISBN 0-87191-254-6

CONTENTS

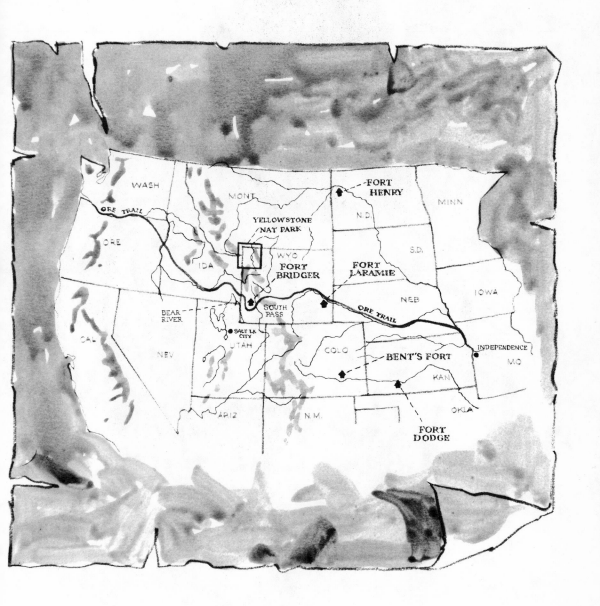

UP THE WILD MISSOURI

Jim Bridger was born in Virginia. The year was 1804, the same time that Lewis and Clark set off to find a route between the Mississippi and the Pacific Ocean. Jim's family moved West in 1812.

For four years, the Bridger family worked a farm in Illinois, just across the

Mississippi from St. Louis. Then Jim's parents died. He hired out to a blacksmith, but he hated the work. In 1822, when he was 18, he signed up with a fur company that was going up the Missouri River. The country up there had been first explored by Lewis and Clark. Now trappers in search of beaver risked death to enter it.

Jim Bridger and the other men rode in keelboats. They poled their way upstream for 1,800 miles, with hostile Indians stealing their herd of horses and threatening their lives. At

the mouth of the Yellowstone River they built a log stockade. It was named Fort Henry. This would be headquarters for the fur trappers, who would range out in all directions seeking the valuable beaver fur.

Jim learned the trade of a mountain man—as the fur trappers were called. He worked outdoors for months on end in all kinds of weather. At night he slept under the open sky. His food was wild game, his drink cold water. And always there were the Indians, ready to rob or even kill.

The beaver fur that Jim risked his life for was sent to England and made into rich men's hats!

As they worked, the mountain men explored the high country. In 1824, Jim Bridger went with a famous trail-blazer, Jedediah Smith, and some other men. They were the first to cross the South Pass from east to west. Later, thousands of settlers would follow them. The path they made, hunting beavers, would become part of the famous Oregon Trail. It would open the Northwest to settlers.

THE INLAND SEA

Next winter, Jim did some single-handed exploring. The trappers were camped along the Bear River. They wondered where the river went.

"I'll find out!" said young Jim Bridger.

He built himself a bull-boat. First he made a frame out of strong saplings. It was shaped like a large bowl. Then he stretched and sewed buffalo hide over the frame. "You're crazy, Jim!" the men said. "What if you go over a waterfall?"

But Jim only grinned. He cut a long pole, got into his boat, and sailed off down the river.

And then he entered the rapids.

The tiny boat whirled through foaming water, crashing into rocks and bouncing off

canyon walls. Jim hung on for his life and wondered if he should jump out. At last the river calmed down. After passing through a marsh, Jim emerged on a great body of water. He tasted it—and it was salt.

"It's the Pacific Ocean!" he exclaimed. But he was wrong. He had discovered Great Salt Lake.

KING OF THE MOUNTAIN MEN

Jim also explored the country that became Yellowstone Park. But when he told
people about the geysers and boiling mud-
holes he had seen there, they called him a
liar!

After a few years, Jim became a "captain"—leading a band of trappers. He became known even among the Indians for his honesty and bravery.

In 1832 there was a fight with Blackfeet Indians and Jim was shot in the back with two arrows. One of them remained in his tough body for two years—until it was removed by the pioneer missionary-surgeon, Dr. Marcus Whitman, who was on his way to Oregon.

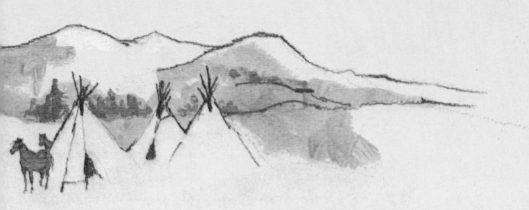

The mountain men built no homes and tilled no farms. They lived like Indians—and many of the western tribes were friendly to them. In 1835, Jim married the daughter of a Flathead chief.

But times were changing. Beaver were scarce now. And even worse, the fashion for beaver hats was dying. Mountain men saw their livelihood slowly crumbling away. Jim wondered what he would do.

The answer came in an unexpected way.

In 1842, he met his old friend, Kit Carson.

Kit was guide to John Charles Fremont, who

was mapping the Oregon Trail. Before long,

the men told Jim, thousands of settlers would

be coming West.

And when they came, they would need supplies and expert advice. Who could furnish them better than Jim Bridger?

He was already famous as "king of the mountain men." In 1843, he and a partner set up Fort Bridger along the Oregon Trail in southwestern Wyoming. It was a great success. Many emigrants passed through it and were helped by Jim. In 1847, he advised Brigham Young, leader of the Mormons, about fertile lands that lay in Utah. The Mormons followed Jim's advice and settled south of the Great Salt Lake he had explored.

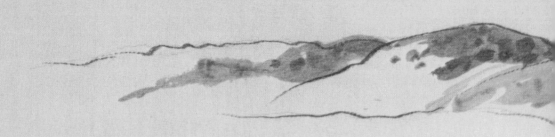

Jim knew personal tragedy during those years. His first wife died, and so did his second. He married Little Fawn, daughter of the Shoshoni chief, Washakie.

In 1850, Utah became a territory of the United States. Brigham Young was its governor. The people of Utah needed money, and Young decided to take over Fort Bridger. Jim was ordered to turn the fort over to new managers. He refused, and Fort Bridger was burned.

TWILIGHT OF A GIANT

Jim took his wife and small children to Missouri. He bought a farm. But there were rumors that the Mormons were in trouble with the government. Jim still hoped that he would some day get his fort back.

In 1856, Jim talked to the President. James Buchanan was planning to send an army into Utah. He felt that the Mormons were rebels. Jim gladly agreed to guide the troops, leaving his family behind.

He was gone for three years. During this time, his wife died, leaving five motherless children. When the trouble with the Mormons was over, the Civil War broke out. And the Indian Wars were starting on the Plains.

Jim found people to look after his children. He went back to scouting for the army. From 1862 to 1868 he guided one expedition after another. For much of that time he was

chief of scouts. Admiring generals claimed that "Jim Bridger had the whole West mapped in his head." But even though he was praised, he was still unable to get his beloved Fort Bridger back. It was taken over by the army.

Jim Bridger retired to his farm in Missouri in 1871, where he lived for the next ten years with his daughters. He was beloved for his story-telling. People could hardly tell where the incredible truth ended and the tall tales began—so fantastic had been his life. When Jim Bridger died in 1881, the West was all but tamed.

And he had helped to do it, for better or worse.

* *
# GALLERY OF GREAT AMERICANS SERIES
* *

INDIANS OF AMERICA
GERONIMO
CRAZY HORSE
CHIEF JOSEPH
PONTIAC
SQUANTO
OSCEOLA

EXPLORERS OF AMERICA
COLUMBUS
LEIF ERICSON
DeSOTO
LEWIS AND CLARK
CHAMPLAIN
CORONADO

FRONTIERSMEN OF AMERICA
DANIEL BOONE
BUFFALO BILL
JIM BRIDGER
FRANCIS MARION
DAVY CROCKETT
KIT CARSON

WAR HEROES OF AMERICA
JOHN PAUL JONES
PAUL REVERE
ROBERT E. LEE
ULYSSES S. GRANT
SAM HOUSTON
LAFAYETTE

WOMEN OF AMERICA
CLARA BARTON
JANE ADDAMS
ELIZABETH BLACKWELL
HARRIET TUBMAN
SUSAN B. ANTHONY
DOLLEY MADISON

* *